How's Everything?

PETER STOKES

Note for Librarians: A cataloguing record for this book is available from Library and Archives Canada at www.collectionscanada.ca/amicus/index-e.html
ISBN 1-4120-6012-5

Printed in Victoria, BC, Canada. Printed on paper with minimum 30% recycled fibre. Trafford's print shop runs on "green energy" from solar, wind and other environmentally-friendly power sources.

PUBLISHING™
Offices in Canada, USA, Ireland and UK
This book was published *on-demand* in cooperation with Trafford Publishing. On-demand publishing is a unique process and service of making a book available for retail sale to the public taking advantage of on-demand manufacturing and Internet marketing. On-demand publishing includes promotions, retail sales, manufacturing, order fulfilment, accounting and collecting royalties on behalf of the author.

Book sales for North America and international:
Trafford Publishing, 6E–2333 Government St.,
Victoria, BC v8t 4p4 CANADA
phone 250 383 6864 (toll-free 1 888 232 4444)
fax 250 383 6804; email to orders@trafford.com
Book sales in Europe:
Trafford Publishing (uk) Limited, 9 Park End Street, 2nd Floor
Oxford, UK ox1 1hh UNITED KINGDOM
phone 44 (0)1865 722 113 (local rate 0845 230 9601)
facsimile 44 (0)1865 722 868; info.uk@trafford.com
Order online at:
trafford.com/05-0913

10 9 8 7 6 5

One diner's personal view on

Tips and tipping

Contents

"How's Everything?"

As a Server:

If you're interested in increasing your personal income then *"How's everything?"* is the one question you should never, ever ask any of your customers

Strike the words from your memory

Become an ex *"How's everything?"* Server

Tell your co-workers to never use that question

Resist the *"How's everything?"* addiction at all times

Be prepared to wean yourself off the *"How's everything?"* question so that you can gain the ability to <u>immediately</u> earn significantly more money

Sound interesting?   **Can you do it?**

... Read on and find out

Acknowledgments

THE 'THANKS' COURSE

In my travels across five continents, I have observed and chatted with countless thousands of people in and around the food service business; Servers, restaurateurs and, more importantly, customers. To all of them I am most grateful, for they have all contributed to this book, albeit mostly unknowingly. However, the value of their input is not diminished by their anonymity.

The following people, however, have been directly responsible in helping me finalize this project and have all used various techniques from gentle support, through determined cajoling, to downright nagging to ensure its completion:

Thanks to Seri Begawaniaka who, many years ago in her restaurant in Kandy, Sri Lanka, sowed the seed in my mind that all servers can significantly increase their earnings, if they wish to do so, by using thoughtful communication skills and a detailed understanding of their customers' needs.

Thanks also to my good friends, Dr. Brian King and his wife Eunice in England, for being the catalysts in launching this particular project one recent summer evening at Victoria's

Inner Harbour in British Columbia, Canada. Their continued support in the transfer of my brain's frustrated ramblings on this topic to the more organized written word is much appreciated.

Thanks, in particular, to Annette Humphries of Trafford Publishing for her unfailing support, countless suggestions and patience with both the technical and creative aspects of the gentle art of authoring.

I am also grateful to Jim Unger, a fellow Vancouver Island resident, whose award-winning syndicated newspaper feature HERMAN® continues to appear in more than 800 daily newspapers worldwide. *Herman®* always seems to 'hit the spot' when it comes to finding the funny side of service, particularly in the restaurant industry. I am most grateful for Jim's permission to reproduce some of his funnier cartoons in this book.

Finally, my thanks and undying gratitude to my wife, Lynnette, to whom I dedicate this book. Lynnette has continually given me her unconditional support and ceaseless encouragement to complete this project, notwithstanding that I was either continually under her feet, or away and 'lost in the book' for days on end.

HERMAN®

by Jim Unger

9-15 © Jim Unger/dist. by United Media, 2001

**"What do I have to do to get
some service around here?"**

Introduction

THE IMPORTANCE OF TIPPING

It was a balmy summer evening a few years back and my wife and I were dining in a not-too-expensive restaurant in Vancouver, BC that we had never visited before. The hors d'ouvres were excellent but, unfortunately, the service was somewhat non-committal and cool. The Server appeared distant and disinterested, not only in her work in general but with us in particular. Now, both Lynnette and I like to 'dine' rather than 'feed' and we always look forward to our dining-out experiences as occasions of relaxing pleasure, so this meal wasn't becoming the best dining-out experience for us, thus far.

The entrée was served – prime rib for Lynnette and salmon for myself, as I remember. Both plates looked delicious, visually well presented and piping hot. The chef had done an excellent job. However, no comment at all came from our Server as she placed (almost plonked!) our meals before us.

Not a word.

Nothing.

A minute later, though, she returned with that unan-swerable question:

"And how's everything?"

You will see, as we progress here that *that question* is the absolutely worst question to ask any diner and should never, ever, ever be uttered. Hard to believe, isn't it, as virtually every Server around the globe asks that question in one language or another of every customer?

Stay with me, though and I'll explain:

*At the time of her asking "**And how's everything?**" neither of us had sampled 'everything' on our plates and neither of us could actually answer her immediately as we were both still busy with our first mouthfuls of food. This left us all very frustrated, particularly as our server continued to hover over our table until I could finish my mouthful sufficiently to answer her question – a 'quality control' question that her employer, no doubt, demanded that she ask each table after each entrée is served.*

What did I answer? Well, by that time, our initial expectations of good service had deteriorated so much that my answer was as meaningless as the question:

"Fine"

I eventually responded – and so the ritual was complete. She was relieved of her duty and able to retreat, her obligation completed.

The final bill, as I remember, was around $105.00 to which I added a nominal 5% gratuity, for the good food quality. This was way below my usual 15% – 20% that I would have been happy to tip, had the experience been more professional and friendly.

That was a lost income opportunity, on the Server's part, of receiving at least $10.50 more – and that's from just one table! If you extend that loss over her work shift, that day, how much more cash did she and her colleagues potentially lose? With a little more thought and attention on the Server's part, our dining experience could have been much more enjoyable and, consequently, her gratuity much higher. Not only would that have translated to higher income for all Servers concerned (pooled gratuity program) but would have gone a long way to encouraging us to revisit that restaurant for another meal in the future – something we won't now do. After all, why would we?

On that occasion, I chose not to complain to the person-in-charge. Although I am in the habit of always commending Servers who give *superlative* service, complaining is not something I frequently do. I usually just vote with my feet. Now, I guess that the Server was quite upset at not receiving a decent tip that evening but was I unfair? Should I have tipped 15+% regardless of the quality of her service?

The way I see it, our Server failed to create a comfortable, friendly and relaxing experience. Why should she be rewarded for that? Once I enter that restaurant, do I assume a responsibility for that Server's income? Of course not. Had I been encouraged by her to tip more generously, it would not only have benefited the Server, it would have meant more money for the other Servers and kitchen staff, all of whom were tied to a pooled gratuity system, as I later found out.

Are there many other people like me who will tip generously for good service yet sometimes leave zero for a bad experience? From conversations I've had on this topic, Servers would like to increase their tips but few of them knew how to upgrade their skills to achieve this. Interestingly, few Servers understood the simple concept of continuous *superlative* service as the easiest way to increase their income – but more on that later.

I'm sure you have all experienced the bad or zero tipper and cursed the customer for being a schmuck – but maybe – was there something that you did, or failed to do, that caused that unsatisfactory ending?

There should <u>never</u> be an occasion for bad or indifferent service and, likewise, customers should <u>never</u> be given the opportunity to justify giving a zero or low percentage gratuity.

Remember:

**The customer is the most important person
in a restaurant**

(It's their money that keeps the restaurant in
business and you in work)

**The Server is the second-most important person
in a restaurant**

(It is your skills that encourage the customers to
part with their money)

*(In fact – don't tell the boss
but he/she is way down this list!)*

Rather like a mathematical equation, you can deduce from this that you cannot survive without customers but your restaurant cannot survive without both customers <u>and you, the Servers.</u>

There are a number of publications that deal with this topic of increasing your tips and I recommend that you research them all for as much information as you can gain on the topic. However, I was not very successful in finding much of value, written from the perspective of the *most important person in the restaurant* – the customer – the diner – **the tipper!**

This, then, is where I'm coming from. I am not a psychologist, psychiatrist or 'psych' anything. I am just a long-time observer of people and a regular dining-out patron. I have a life-long passion with food and people and have had the very fortunate opportunity of experiencing this passion in many continents around the globe.

I have mostly basic expectations of an eating establishment but I don't see my needs fully satisfied in many places that I visit. That's why I have written this book. After all, it is my money you are taking and – don't get me wrong – I'm quite happy to part with more money if I'm encouraged to do so. I will tip well when I receive good food and *superlative* service. It costs the Server no extra money and only a very little extra time and effort to change bad service to good service to *superlative service.* Now, you may not have much control over the quality and presentation of the food on the plate. However, you do have control over the rest – and that's what this book is all about.

You may think my reasons for publishing this book are purely self-serving. Well, you are right. My thoughts are that if you are able to earn more money from your customers then it naturally means that your customers have a heightened satisfaction level – and that means me too!!

Above all, I would love to dine in a restaurant without ever hearing that 'dreaded question' again. Too much to hope for? Well, that's up to you.

There are university professors who will show you in great statistical detail how one behavioural trait will give you a finite percentage tip-increase over another behavioural trait – and that's good. These surveys should be researched and read by all. You will be able to read articles from Wait Staff Trainers, who have many differing ideas on how to heighten your skills as a Server – and they're good as well. Lastly, you will be able to join various internet chat rooms and blog sites where experiences can be aired on common problems that Servers experience. Become involved. Any fresh ideas that can increase your income should be welcomed.

Consider your own approach to customers and honestly think whether you ask yourself directly any of these questions at the time you meet them:

- "Why has this customer chosen this restaurant?"

- "What does this customer really want?"

- "What's important to this customer?"

This book, then, is one such customer's answer to these and other very important questions that may just give you the clue to giving *superlative* customer service.

Whatever terminology preference you have for your work position, I have chosen to use the term *'Server'* to cover all and have deliberately stayed gender-neutral throughout this book. My main purpose is to show you how to increase your income, regardless of gender, age or culinary ability.

It is generally recognized that some communication techniques are better suited to females whilst others are easier for males to master. It doesn't take an 'Einstein' to figure these out, by and large, so I won't be spending any time separating the techniques for gender preference. I will try and show you that it is your 'connection' and 'communicative ability' with the diner that mostly influences the level of tips you receive.

My experience has been more as an itinerate traveller, dining at different restaurants, for the most part. However, do not forget about the regular diners. They can be most important:

A Server friend of mine once told me that she always welcomes the regular diner and one, she recalled in particular, always asks for her by name, sits at her table and always tips a five dollar bill.

Not a great percentage in relation to his tab but he comes in three times a week without fail for his meals and, when multiplied by 52 weeks a year, his tips more than pay for the Server's annual car insurance premium.

She told me that, as a result of striving to keep this regular diner, she has learned a lot about giving a consistently high level of customer service and this has served her very well with all her customers.

This is not a book that will teach you the mechanics of how to serve food, pour wine or clear tables. It is about the thinking and communication skills needed to better please your diners, thereby raising your earnings through increased gratuities.

This book is unashamedly, about you, the Server, and how to make more money for yourself – pure and simple.

Throughout this book I make constant connections to customers' attitudes and responses and how each communication may affect the final gratuity. This is designed to show you how frequently, throughout a meal, you have the opportunity to affect the final outcome. It's not just the big smile at the end of the meal, as you present the bill, with a

hope-against-hope-fingers-crossed-praying-to-the-heavens-eyes-squeezed-tight-shut wish for a big tip.

It should be a continual and planned strategy, designed to encourage the 'bill payer', subconsciously, to <u>want</u> to leave more money for you. It is irrelevant whether you are serving at the finest of dining establishments or the most basic of cafes. Where gratuities are involved, you have a very simple opportunity of significantly increasing your tips – if you wish to take it.

Now, as we all know, there is a direct correlation between happy, relaxed and satisfied diners and the size of their gratuities! The concepts are simple – By tuning your thought processes, your verbal skills and your body language to your customers' needs and expectations, dining experiences can be dramatically enhanced.

If, at your location, gratuities are pooled then it will certainly be in your financial interest to share the information in this book with the rest of your team. Better still, have everyone buy their own book. Bring it to the attention of the owner so that all Servers can become familiar with these techniques and use them in a concerted effort to ensure that everyone gains financially.

In addition, it is certainly in your management's interest for you to receive more money. They will love to have happier customers without it costing them any extra money or time. Perhaps you can even convince your management to buy this book for each Server as an encouragement for everyone to become more efficient.

In fact, anything at all that will increase your customers' satisfaction will increase your income and be welcomed by all.

You will be able to easily understand the concepts and apply them without changing too many of your current habits. Mind you, if some of your usual habits are changed as a result of applying the concepts in this book and higher income results, how bad can that be? After all, the more successful your working establishment, as a result of your efforts, the more in demand your services will become and the higher your basic income will become as well. In other words – If you're *superlative*, Management will want you around more often.

Your reward, most importantly, will be extra cash. Additionally, though, with this success may also come greater job satisfaction and who would say no to that?

At this stage, if you'd classify yourself as a 'doubting Thomas' and are cynical as to whether you can significantly raise your level of tips then all I can say is –

Don't knock it until you've tried it.

In my world, that advice is right up there with Nike's

'Just Do It'

as the two most important pieces of advice to any ambitious person about virtually anything.

On the other hand, if there's one amongst you who says to your customers or employer:

"Please do not tip me. I don't want the money.
Give any extra cash I make to someone else."

then just pass this book to another Server who is from this planet!

Quite simply, if you'd like to increase your earning power, at virtually no cost or time to you, then this book is about you and for you: You as an individual and you as a team member.

HERMAN®

**"I'll have a table for you,
Sir, in just two minutes."**

The Customer

THE MOST IMPORTANT PERSON IN THE HOUSE

This may sound simple but it's often forgotten that:

You are there for your diners' benefit – not the other way round.

Pun intended, your diners are your 'bread and butter' and it would help immensely to understand their motives and behaviour-patterns a little better. After all, it is the customer's perception that's all-important when it comes to evaluating good service. The customer is the one who pays the bill, decides on the amount of the tip and then pays it! By 'knowing' your customers better and relating to them more effectively you will become more professional and raise the opportunity for a higher gratuity, which, after all, is what it's all about.

As you may know, the most commonly accepted acronym for **TIPS** is:

'To Insure Proper (or Prompt) Service'.

Originally, customers paid tips in advance as an insurance against slow, bad or indifferent service, not to mention ques-

21

tionable food quality. I always think of this as a form of bribery, by today's standards, although many a wise ocean cruise passenger will still tip in advance, or at least partially in advance, to be sure of a very comfortable, well-attended voyage.

Nowadays, with the tip payment at the end of the meal, the amount is now a reflection of the diner's satisfaction, not anticipation. Consequently, there's only one person who can affect that reward directly – and that's you, the Server.

The other anomaly in today's world is the dining establishment where a fixed gratuity is demanded, in print, right in the menu. Personally, whenever I'm to pay the bill, I do my best to avoid these locations. My experience has shown that, wherever incentive has been taken away in any customer service industry, customer service inevitably suffers. I realize this is a rather large generalization. However, I cannot argue with my own life's experiences.

I recently visited Victoria, BC for a business meeting and was taken to a restaurant where a fixed 15% gratuity was stated on the menu.

> *We were greeted very well at the reception desk, ushered to our seat professionally but that was where the customer service seemed to stop.*
>
> *The meals were excellent but the service stunk!*
>
> *We didn't even receive a visit to the table after our entrees were served to be asked that forbidden question "How's Everything?"*
>
> *My business partner was paying and, when presented with the bill, strongly resented having to pay the fixed gratuity to a Serving team that were merely going through the motions.*
>
> *There was no use in complaining, though, as the problem wasn't solely with one Server but was systemic*

throughout the whole system at that location. Next time,
we shall obviously go elsewhere.
Quite sad, actually, as the artistry from the kitchen
was mouth-watering to view and delicious to taste.

Should you be working in one of these 'fixed-gratuity' locations, the principles espoused in this book can still help in tempting your diners to add that extra tip that a really enjoyable time can often bring forward. It may be, under those circumstances, that any extra gratuities will flow directly to you so the incentive for *superlative* service will remain paramount.

Whatever your thoughts are on this matter, the fact remains that the vast majority of diners, in this world, wait to the very end of their relationship with their Server before deciding what that Server and the food was worth, in financial terms. This may sound a little clinical but it's true. At the end of their meal, your customer will place a monetary value on your services, based usually as a percentage, on the final bill total.

Why wait to the end and rely solely on your customer's dreaded decision, when you can begin to influence that customer evaluation from the very moment you introduce yourself to them? When a customer enters or is placed at one of your tables all your senses must immediately work and work very quickly to evaluate and understand just what type of people you'll be serving. Consider asking yourself these questions:

Who are they?

Who will be paying?

Why are they here?

Where are they from?

What are their needs?

These are not always simple questions to answer. However, by concentrating on them right at the beginning and forming an impression of just who they are can mean a difference to their increased satisfaction and their gratitude to you.

WHO ARE THEY?

You have seen it all. You know what I'm talking about.

Your next table to serve may be a pair of gruff lawyers who want privacy to discuss a confidential case, a flamboyant entertainer who needs everyone to admire and fawn, a frazzled mom with two scrappy children in tow who just needs French fries and jello for the kids with something 'non-fattening' for herself, a business man with his 'secretary' who wants privacy but *"keep the drinks coming"*, a party of six who like to party and vow to drink the place dry or a quiet in-love couple, looking gooey-eyed at each other over a mutual glass of iced tea, with two straws and completely oblivious to their surroundings.

I'm sure you are all familiar with these types and, indeed, others not mentioned here.

The important thing is that, other than their common desire to eat, they each have their separate needs. The more you are able to identify and understand their needs the easier your job will be. It naturally follows that, if you can cater to their specific needs the more comfortable a customer will feel and the more grateful they will be.

The lawyers, for instance, almost certainly will require a booth or be placed in the most private location with only short interruptions for you to receive their menu orders, serve their choices, etc. More often than not, they will know what they want and need quiet efficiency with little or no interruptions. In communicating with them, use words that they are more likely to use themselves. They don't make "good" menu choices, they make "wise" menu choices. They don't drink wine that "goes with their meal" they "select a wine that will complement their entrée choice". They will appreciate short-comment interruptions such as "excellent" and "very appropriate" when discussing food choices. In addition, always read back their order to them, prior to leaving their table. (Reading back menu orders is, in fact, a crucial need on every occasion but more of this later.) They will appreciate your thoroughness, attention to detail and correctness. It's just who they are.

The frazzled mom, however, will need someone to look after her children while she's there and would love 'something special' for herself. Suggest or even make 'something special' and see the result. She'll love it. The more interruptions and support you can give her the better for her. You will also have to make a judgement call whether the kids are mature enough to make their own menu choices, in which case they should be individually and directly addressed. They will feel more 'grown-up' and the mom will feel that you appreciate her children more as individuals. She will be most grateful for not having to be the 'go-between' all the time. If in doubt, ask the mom whether you can take their orders direct. She will value your interest.

The businessman with his 'secretary' needs his privacy too but also needs to be treated as an important man in the eyes of his 'company'. Again, his food choices should be complimented but with a little more attention than the lawyers, mentioned before.

I could go on but these different needs are not too difficult to assess and you should adapt your approach and communication style to suit each particular customer need. Again, you need to think of your approach right from the very beginning when you first meet them. Make a judgement on their needs and adjust your perceptions as you get to know them better.

For instance, I clearly remember an incident in a select restaurant in Seattle, Washington, a few years ago:

I was having lunch with a business colleague when a flamboyantly dressed middle-aged man entered and loudly instructed the Server to join two tables together as he was expecting to entertain a large group of guests. This was done and he sat at the end of one of the tables, ordered a large vodka tonic and waited.

Seeing him there, I recall thinking what a crass, loud-mouthed man he was and was quite concerned for the future of our quiet business lunch. The last thing I wanted was to be disturbed by the boorish antics of this man and his guests.

However, we needn't have worried.

After about fifteen minutes, not one of his guests had arrived and he started to make urgent "where are you?" calls on his cell phone – obviously with no satisfactory response. The Server was very patient, though and brought him a second, drink but didn't pester him, further. About 20 minutes later a highly embarrassed young 'office boy' turned up (perhaps as a token 'sacrificial lamb'), consumed a coke and a green salad then, after a little embarrassed small talk with the man, left the restaurant.

It became obvious that whomever he had invited had no intentions of having lunch with him on that day. He was left stranded in the middle of a busy restaurant, sitting at the head of two laid-up but empty tables, having made a grandiose entrance and now covered in humiliating embarrassment.

The Server was brilliant, though. About ten minutes after the young man had scurried out, she approached the man with a note in her hand and stated, quite loudly, that the brokers he was to have lunched with had suffered a complete electrical breakdown and fire in their office, that a special messenger at the front door would give him more details and would he follow her to the entrance.

The man, extremely relieved to have been released from his 'prison' on 'center stage', followed the Server to the entrance and out of our sight.

Having observed this in detail, I was curious to know what had happened and approached the Server on leaving the restaurant at the end of our meal. She confided that the story she'd told the man was a complete fabrication but he was so relieved at being extricated from the restaurant 'honourably' that he paid for his drinks and the salad then tipped her a $100 bill in gratitude for her rescuing him.

The point, here, is that the Server could have separated the tables, cleared away the extra cutlery and water glasses, re-positioned the chairs then demanded he order something from the menu or leave as this was the busy lunch period. However, she recognized the man for what he was, understood the situation he had put himself in when no-one turned up to dine with him and expertly <u>looked after his needs</u>.

The man, in an obviously rare moment of sensitivity, felt his honour was saved and was very grateful. In addition, he probably left the establishment comfortable enough to be able to return on another occasion.

In my view, the Server was a genius.

WHO WILL BE PAYING?

Firstly and most importantly, you should determine, as best you can and as soon as possible, who will be paying for the meal. The reason that this is of the utmost importance is that:

The one who pays, most often, is the one who tips!

When a family enters it is relatively easy to decide who will be paying as, more often than not, it's the 'dominant' male (nothing sexist intended) who will be paying. There are many combinations of people who dine together, though and, if you're unable to decide, an initial question at the beginning of the encounter should always determine whether 'separate checks' will be required.

If, however, separate checks are not requested and it isn't specifically made clear who will be picking up the tab, then you must make your best judgement as to who will be paying. This need not be as difficult as it seems. Body language interpretation is such an important tool for you that the next chapter is devoted entirely to the subject.

Here, though, we will stick to finding who the 'leader' is and, therefore, who will be providing the gratuity. This is crucial as the 'leader' is the most important person in a group, whether the group consists of only two people or twenty-two.

In effect, more often than not, it is the 'leader' who controls the meal. Other members of the group will not over order without specific permission and will often defer to the 'leader' on how expensive an item they can order. The bigger the group, the more important this criteria becomes. If the 'leader' elects to order a starter then more of the group will follow suit. If the question of starters is left in the air for all to answer independently, you will always notice some reticence to order by those not close to the 'leader'. If you have guessed the 'leader' correctly and identified with him/her the more popular starters that are available you are more likely to achieve additional starter orders if the 'leader' chooses to have one. Prompting is always a good strategy. Likewise with beverages, particularly at lunchtimes, the 'leader' will usually dictate, by ordering his/her own, whether the beverages will be alcoholic or not.

Never forget that your tip is usually calculated as a percentage of the total bill so it will be in your interests to up-sell your diners as much as is reasonable unless, of course it would be more expedient for you to consider table turn-rounds as an off-setting strategy for busier times.

The dynamics of the actual people also come into play. A gentleman will rarely criticize the ordering of an expensive item by his sole female companion, unless, of course, it is his wife – just a quirk of human nature, I suppose but an important one to pick up on, nonetheless.

It is important that the remainder of the group be treated with courtesy and friendliness but you must always pay special attention to the payer and defer to the payer as the 'leader' of the pack'. As with most other species of mammals, human beings are no different in that we have leaders and we have followers. You will notice that 'leaders' usually have a heightened level of self-confidence, stand 'tall' and don't assume a hunched or slouched position either standing or sitting. They will also make quick decisions, for themselves and for the group, as a whole, if necessary.

In today's society, 'leader of the pack' is not an exclusive male domain. There is now a much healthier balance of leaders between the genders so be careful not to assume, too quickly, that the male in the group at your table is the 'leader'. A mistake, here, could reverse the final outcome of what you are trying to achieve. It is here that your experience with understanding body language will help you immensely.

It is my experience that females, in a 'leader's' position, are not so consumed with ego and feelings of self-importance, unlike many of their male counterparts. Your customer service skills, therefore, may be more keenly reviewed at the time of bill presentation. Just a thought.

In the microcosm of life that your restaurant becomes, you should always recognize the 'leader of the pack' in any group and, unless they have made a prior declaration of 'equality' by requesting separate checks, the 'leader' should always receive special attention throughout the meal. This is not to say that others should be ignored. However, the 'leader' should be made to feel important, his/her advice sought, preferences requested and satisfied. After all, the 'leader' will be awarding you your gratuity, independently, without consulting the 'followers' around him/her.

It is to the 'leader' you should subsequently and personally enquire of the quality of the meal served. It is also to the 'leader' that you should ask if you may remove the emptied plates of the other group members from the table, during the course of the meal. Being an every-day occurrence in Europe, this practice may sound a little odd in North America. However, it will certainly show the 'leader' that you are looking to him/her for guidance throughout the meal. For those of you in North America, you'll be surprised how this technique will enamour you to the 'leaders' and, usually, they'll be very appreciative of your courtesy and deference to their position.

In addition, never 'just' go through the process of pouring the initial taste of wine for the 'leader'. As a Server, you should always ask the 'leader', specifically and in front of his/her 'group', if he/she would prefer to taste the wine. The 'leader' will then take the opportunity of deciding whether to accept this leadership role, delegate the task to one of the group or simply allow you to pour for everyone else without the formal tasting ceremony. In fact, many 'leaders' now feel more power in waiving off this largely symbolic act (with apologies to the sommeliers amongst you). It is attention to these small points that will bring you closer, symbiotically, to the 'leader'.

There is a feeling of self-importance in all leaders and we can see many examples if we just look at our royalty, politicians, company executives, show business personalities, athletes, etc. The feeling of self-importance is often connected with the need for recognition of their power. In more traditional times, we elevated our leaders to give them a higher profile. They sat on large, ornate thrones, wore high, glittery hats (crowns), rode in large carriages drawn by more horses than anyone else could afford and generally lived in adulation by their followers.

However, in these modern times and in the relatively non-combative and less excessive environment of your restaurant, these shows of authority are usually satisfied by mere recognition of their status and you, as servers, have the ability of making their leadership qualities shine to their immediate dining group, in particular and the restaurant population as a whole.

Bear in mind, the 'leader' can achieve very little for his group, in your restaurant, without you. It truly is a team effort and you should capitalize on the 'leader's' needs. Few of the followers will recognize your tactics but the 'leaders' will and will be most grateful – particularly the electable ones!

With all that I have said on 'leaders' I don't mean to infer that other diners should be ignored. Far from it as you should keep a high level of attentiveness to all diners. However, the 'leader' will be giving you your gratuity. Ensure that he/she stays on your team!

Should separate checks be required, then your work is cut out for you, as I'm sure you already know.

It will be necessary for you to achieve a personal relationship with each diner if you want to maximize the gratuities from your group. It's hard work, I know but never show it to be a chore when separate checks are requested as it offers you a chance to influence each individual diner to be generous. Humour is always a good starter when separate checks are requested and, in a humorous vein, it sometimes helps to emphasize to each diner the extra work you will have to do.

You now have the chance to treat each diner as equally important and individually special – and you should.

A wise Server once told me that he looked forward to large groups where separate checks were requested.

He said that this gave him a wonderful opportunity to identify each of the persons' needs, work individually with each person's personality, on occasion, play one off against another and, consequently, create a very positive relationship with each of them. The Server confided that this tended to create a very positive attitude and "good vibe atmosphere" amongst all the diners. As a result of this "good vibe atmosphere", each one of the group seemed much more comfortable in leaving a higher-than-normal tip.

Now, it's fair to say that this Server was a very friendly sort of guy but even he admitted to having had to practice these skills many times before he finally 'got it right'. His last comment, though, was that it was certainly worth it and the level of his tips, under these circumstances, increased dramatically.

From my point of view, as a diner, I love to be recognized, treated as an individual (even in a group scenario) and I appreciate those personal touches that only a thoughtful Server can give.

William Shakespeare wrote in 'As You Like It' that "All the World's a stage and men and women merely players." He must have been thinking of his experiences in Elizabethan taverns at the time as each modern-day Server's work shift is one of theatrical proportions. You overcome, or capitalize, on your personal feelings and emotions of the day and strive to give diners *superlative* customer service.

Professional actors could do well to study your work and copy your example.

WHY ARE THEY HERE?

Ever since Neanderthal hunters stopped at convenient bushes in the forest to snack on berries during the hunt, man (and now woman) has needed locations to eat to maintain their energy until they return to their 'mud huts' at the end of each day. Nowadays, the reasons for dining-out have expanded past the 'berry' stage, although, for all diners, being your guests for a meal is <u>always</u> an alternative to their regular home experience.

It will be very beneficial for you to find out why your customers have come to your restaurant and your communication style with them should vary to cater to each rationale.

If your customers are using their dining table as an extension of their boardroom then they will likely not require too many interruptions and familiarity. However, a couple having a celebratory anniversary dinner will want to be looked after like 'royalty'. This is their treat for you to organize. Unlike home, they have the choice of all the menu options, they can order whatever they wish to drink and they do not have to clear away and wash the dishes afterwards. Your relaxed friendliness will go a long way to ensuring that they have a great time with you.

The atmosphere at the table will be considerably different for the celebratory couple than for the business people and it will be very much to your benefit to be very sensitive to these differences and adapt to them quickly and completely.

No matter why they are at your table, try to avoid initiating your communication with *"and how are you today?"* Sure, it's a greeting and not meant to be taken as a genuine concern for their health. BUT – You will sound just like the anonymous telephone solicitor collecting for a similarly anonymous charity who always seems to call your home at meal times – Ring too many alarm bells?

Why not try something more personal:

> *"Hi. I'm Elizabeth and I'm glad you came here, this*
> *evening. Have you visited our restaurant before?"*

If you ask opened-ended questions, at this stage, it will invite direct and maybe chatty answers that you can build on to cement this new relationship. If you just ask the old favorite *"and how are you today?"* you will only get back that regular mean-nothing one-syllable word *"Fine."* End of conversation and a waste of a good relationship-building opportunity.

Then you might follow up with:

> *"Just make yourselves comfortable. Here are your*
> *menus and I'll be right back to look after your drinks."*

By using this or similar openings you will have immediately personalized the occasion for them with real conversation, not worn-out clichés and ensuring them time to settle and get comfortable – just like home, perhaps. Also, by using language that you feel your customers are more used to hearing in their everyday life, the more comfortable they will be with you, the more affinity they will feel for you and the closer your relationship will be with them.

You will notice that I have underlined the personal pronouns in each Server quotation throughout this book. This is to highlight the importance of personalizing yourself, your food and your service to your diner.

Read those last two quoted sentences again, then compare their effectiveness against the following greeting sentence:

"Coffee?"

Get my drift?

The more you personalize yourself, your food and your service the more your customer will bond to you.

The importance of introducing yourself by name cannot be overstated. There have been so many studies, both in Europe and North America, which have shown that the use of 'legible' nametags and/or verbal use of names in introductions dramatically increases tips. In fact, I have yet to read a survey where only a marginal increase in tips has been recorded.

Believe me, this is very powerful.

Speaking as a diner, I always know I'm going to have an enjoyable time at the table when my Server highlights the initial greeting as being *special* and then gives me (and my fellow guests) a little time to settle before asking for decisions on drinks, food choices, etc. I've also often found that, if the greeting was 'powerful' and we are given a little time to settle, we often find ourselves commenting on the friendly start to the meal. That means we are confirming amongst ourselves the positive first impression created by the Server. We then automatically look on his/her next appearance in a much more friendly manner.

Although I deal with this at greater length in the chapter on Body Language, whenever you are introducing yourself to a guest, ensure that you always make direct eye contact with them. This is a strong indicator of your friendly nature and will encourage similar intimacy on their part.

If you are able to identify the 'leader' and engage him/her in direct eye contact, this will initiate your working relationship right from the very start.

WHERE ARE THEY FROM?

Whether they are *"here on business"*, *"vacationing"* or just *"passing through"* your customers always seem to think more of their home town when they are away from it so you should, if possible, find a common bond with their hometown or area.

If you've been to their hometown, know someone who has or have any personal knowledge of their area you should comment on it. Even saying *"I hear it's beautiful"* or *"You certainly have a great football team in your town"* will help cement a bond and make them feel acknowledged and appreciated.

I remember an occasion in a restaurant just outside Dallas, Texas, one of the largest of the American States:

> *An elderly couple came in and, rather timidly, sat at a table, seemingly over-awed by everything around them. The Server approached them, obviously noted they were 'not from around these parts' and enquired where they were from.*
>
> *The husband rather apprehensively said "Canada!" to which the Server responded in her broadest Texan accent,*
>
> *"Why, isn't that country such a size that it's bigger than the whole of the United States?"*
>
> *Now, I doubt that their actual hometown was much bigger than the restaurant they were seated in but the*

Server had won them over immediately and they visibly relaxed, having a great time for the rest of their visit. I don't know what level of gratuity was left with the Server but I can guess that it was far greater than if she hadn't made them feel so comfortable, so far from home.

If your guests were locals, then you'll have lots to talk about as long as you stay away from politics, religion and capital punishment. I find that, by staying well away from these three potentially explosive topics, your opinions will be generally acceptable and will help to cement your personal relationship with them. You will also have the opportunity to ensure that they return on a subsequent occasion. All it requires is *superlative customer service!*

WHAT ARE THEIR NEEDS?

As we have discussed already, diners' needs vary according to who they are, their age, their social level, the company they are with and the reason they have chosen to dine out, rather than eat at home. However, if you can identify and satisfy their needs, your diners can feel almost as comfortable as if they are at home. After all, eating a home-cooked meal, surrounded by all the familiar domestic comforts, will always take a lot of beating.

Basic needs, such as whether your customers are in a hurry or, like me most often, wanting to take their time and savor the occasion is always an important first need to identify. For me, confirmation from my Server that a relaxed extended mealtime is okay with them too is a good first step towards a friendly working relationship for the duration of the dinner or lunch.

Your customer's sociability is also important. Unfortunately, there are some customers out there who just don't want to talk or be friendly, no matter how bubbly you are. This doesn't mean that there will be no tip at the end of the service. It just means that you, as their Server, will have to work more creatively on your style of *superlative* customer service. If you are convinced that they are not going to be friendly then, instead of creating open-ended questions that need a detailed response, just communicate with closed questions or statements that require only a "yes", "no" or a grunt!

Don't forget that it's not your job to change their personality. It's your job to create as big a gratuity for yourself as possible when they pay their bill.

I asked a Server friend of mine, recently, what her strategy was under these circumstances and she was very clear in what she did:

> *Being a very sociable, friendly Server, she is always the 'life and soul' of the restaurant but when she identified the 'grumps' (as she called them) at her table, she shed her outgoing personality and communicated in simple closed but friendly statements. This style invariably put them at ease then she sprinkled her communications with small personal compliments such as:*
>
> *"Wise choice of entree"*
>
> *"You certainly know your wines"*
>
> *"I like your tie".*
>
> *By using these little compliments, my Server friend said she gradually instilled in her customers a feeling of acceptance and an unspoken kind of 'kinship' that allowed them to feel at ease.*

Once you have achieved this, they will be relaxed and there will be no reason why your expertise will not be recognized during that final minute when the bill is paid and the gratuity awarded.

At that stage you should be confident that whatever could have been done has been done to assure a maximum gratuity.

HERMAN®

© Jim Unger/dist. by United Media, 1999

"GET YOUR ELBOWS OFF THE TABLE!"

Body Language

IF YOU ONLY PICK UP WHAT IS SAID ALOUD, YOU ARE MISSING HALF THE MESSAGE

Body language – that ever-present type of communication that most people tend to ignore. The study of body language, however, will tell you most of you want to know, if you look and consider the signs that all bodies give out.

Servers, as a group, are probably the most renowned for understanding and interpreting body language. Not only will a quick study identify the 'leader' of your table (and the one who will pay the bill), it will indicate all the various dynamics of the group at the table: Who likes whom, who can't stand whom and who will, most likely, take whom home after the meal!

Also known by its scientific name 'Kinesics', body language for us humans is our original language and significantly predates our current verbal techniques. As far as we know, body language is still the main method of communication practiced by many mammalian sub-species who have yet to attempt, let alone perfect, verbal communication. I think we can learn a lot from them – that is, before we eat them all!

It would be very easy, here, to launch into the whole in-depth subject of body language, as it certainly is a vital key to human communication, however, that is for another time. Unlike verbal communication, body language is rarely deceptive and can be relied upon, more often than our spoken word, to convey true feelings and/or concerns.

> *The clearest example I can give of this is when you have just placed your customer's entrée before him and he is still sitting there with his arms tightly folded across his chest, his chin firmly directed to the floor and eyebrows resembling a freshly ploughed field.*
>
> *Thoughtlessly, you ask him the question, "How's everything?" and he replies "Fine". Now, if you look at him, it doesn't take a top mensa achiever to realize that his body language is telling you one thing and his verbal response another.*

Let's just hope this customer is not calculating your tip in that state!

It is, therefore, very important in your quest for greater understanding of your customer's needs, that by interpreting their body language correctly you will give yourself the opportunity to ask the right question in the right manner to receive the right answer.

Through factual knowledge, in a court of law, an experienced lawyer will never ask a question that he doesn't already know the answer to. Similarly, in a restaurant, if you are aware of many of the body language signals given by diners, you will be able to ask your questions with much greater effect and to the point. Below, are just a few examples illustrating just how easy this can be:

a) You see a waiting diner furtively glance at his/her watch – You offer:
"Are you in a hurry? I'll see if our chef can expedite your order."

b) Your dining couple never stop gazing lovingly at each other – You offer:
"Our crème brulee is truly decadent. May I bring you one to share?"

c) You see a diner gently push his, now empty, plate away from him and lean back in his chair with a satisfied look on his face – Take credit and offer:
"Our Chef certainly seems to have hit the spot with your meal."

Perhaps the best and quickest route to understanding the power of body language is to visit a busy passenger airport and spend some time 'people watching'. You will quickly learn how to identify:

- the body language of an anxious relative waiting for their loved one to emerge through the arrival gate

- the rather subdued woman about to bid farewell to her business-travelling husband

- the excitement of a couple of children waiting to board their first flight

You will also notice the importance of props for some people:

- the matching luggage and furs of a wealthy lady who needs to show others how important she is (or thinks she is)

- the ubiquitous briefcase of the business man being carried swiftly through the Terminal

- the timid first-time traveller, nervously clutching her purse to her chest as she awaits her boarding announcement

- even the macho armed guards swaggering along with their sub-machine guns, as if to demonstrate their ultimate power

These situations easily translate to your workplace and you will learn circumstances where you'll not offer to divest some customers of their props as, to them, it would be like stripping them of their public image.

The whole of life can be seen here and, most of the people can be correctly identified without hearing a single spoken word. By noting people's gestures, actions and how they relate to each other in a physical way you will be able to quite easily assess those peoples' attitudes, relationships and situations.

Learn to tune into body language as you initially approach the table. Communicate from what gestures you see, not necessarily from what you hear. Have you ever wondered how it is that an experienced car salesman can close a customer into exactly the car the customer really likes? It's certainly not because the customer says, *"Yes. This blue one is for me. Sell it to me."* The salesman reads all the customer's body signals that betray his desires, personality, emotions, etc., and guides the relationship, through a number of routes, culminating, of course, in the sale of the blue one! It's no different for you, the Server, except that you're selling steaks, not Chevrolets.

By applying body language techniques, you will have tuned in to the vast world of non-verbal communication that even surpasses verbal communication in most cases. In other words, you have begun to understand body language and how it speaks to us.

Perhaps the best example of body language, from my own experience, came a few years back:

> I was driving to a colleague's home to discuss a business matter when, about one block from his house, I saw a man in the distance walking along the sidewalk. I was immediately struck by his likeness to the friend I was driving to visit but something was different.
>
> As I drew nearer, I could see that it was my friend but his body language drew a completely different picture of him than the happy-go-lucky man that I was going to meet. His hands were thrust deeply into his pockets, with shoulders slouched forward and head bowed. Even his steps dragged along the pavement as he aimlessly kicked at the occasional small pebble along his way. Not the sprightly man I was used to seeing, at all.
>
> I drew up beside him and immediately noticed his 'hang dog' look, with hooded eyes and expressionless, empty face.
>
> Being a fellow Englishman, I immediately knew the appropriate first-aid required and said "Come on. Let's have a pint!" Over our ensuing meeting the 'earth-shattering' catastrophe was merely a hiccough in his love life that was subsequently soon remedied. However, the power of the many body language symbols I received warned me that an insensitive initial greeting could have been disastrous and may have made matters much worse.

Eye Contact

Chapter 11 of Julius Fast's book, entitled "Body Language" is called *"Winking, Blinking and Nods"*. This delightful title encapsulates the topic of eye contact very well. Communicating with the eyes is, perhaps, the purest and most honest form of communication that exists. Julius Fast says:

> *"Of all the parts of the human body that are used to transmit information, the eyes are the most important and can transmit the most subtle nuances. Does this contradict the fact that the eyes do not show emotion? Not really. While the eyeball itself shows nothing, the emotional impact of the eyes occurs because of their use and the use of the face around them.*
>
> *The reason they have so confounded observers is because by length of glance, by opening of the eyelids, by squinting and by a dozen little manipulations of the skin and eyes, almost any meaning can be sent out."*

Eyes are not 'kind', 'wise', 'angry' or anything other than eyes. However, being the 'windows of our souls' they do tend to betray exactly what is in the mind and, as such, can be extremely useful in interpreting just what is in your customer's mind.

The Spanish philosopher, Jose Ortega y Gasset spoke of *"the look"* as something that comes from within *"with the straight line accuracy of a bullet."* *"Every look"*, Ortega says, *"tells us what goes on inside the person who gives it."*

It is often said that eyes will have a conversation with other eyes all on their own and I'm sure we've all had experiences of this. No words have been spoken but by meeting another's eyes, volumes have been communicated. Sounds poetic but it's sometimes just like that.

Can you remember your first true love and the eye-contact feelings there?

Can you remember those stern glances from a parent that immediately stopped our little 'criminal' activities?

You should use this to your advantage and ensure that you gain direct eye contact with every customer you communicate with, particularly the 'leaders' as discussed earlier. Your customers will have great difficulty in saying "no" to any reasonable suggestion you may make when you are engaging them eye-to-eye in a friendly manner.

Eye contact is also very important as an up-selling technique, particularly with desserts, which are often thought of as a tough sell for weight-conscious or penny-conscious diners.

Hold their eyes. Smile. Who could resist?

I should also mention that eye contact is also important with <u>all</u> customers, not just your own. Servers are sometimes renowned for having 'tunnel vision' for their tables only. Speaking as a frequent diner, I cannot see the invisible boundaries you sometimes work within and can get quite frustrated when all I want is a fill of my water glass but no passing Server will meet my glance. Well, you know the rest. As mentioned in the *Introduction,* teamwork is important and it's what helps to set aside the better restaurants and the better Servers.

I have a sneaky feeling there may be some Server training, out there, that specifically suggests 'tunnel vision' in favor of assigned tables to be a good thing. I can tell you that, from the customer's point of view, it is very frustrating and, while I like to be welcome at my particular table I would much prefer to feel welcome in the whole establishment. General eye contact will help do that.

Do not be offended, though, if a diner declines to engage you in eye contact. There are some cultures that don't follow the New World habit of direct eye contact. It means different things to different people. However, other sub-conscious body language traits will still be evident for you to continue to assess.

TOUCHING

Political correctness and modern-day society seem to inhibit touching by strangers and encourage your personal zone as a 'no-go-zone-under-pain-of-death'. However, human beings are naturally tactile, as are most mammals within their own sub-species, and I feel that appropriate touching, in most cases, can dramatically enhance your abilities of creating a close, yet proper, relationship with your diners. This can be particularly effective when dealing with the 'separate check' scenario, where you are working that much harder to establish a relationship with each separate diner.

In fact, it is a commonly held theory that by touching a person you intensify the message you are giving by 300%.

Now that is dramatic!

Non-invasive touching areas include the shoulder, the elbow and the forearm. Obviously, you're not going to go in search of an appropriate body-part unless it's immediately accessible and then only at the right time to accentuate your message. Perhaps the most effective touching strategy is to touch your diner on the shoulder as you are presenting the bill. The shoulder because that is the most available, appropriate and non-invasive part of the body of a sitting diner. The presentation of the bill will detract from any negative connotation and, as long as the touch is for no longer than three seconds, it will not consciously be perceived as invasive but merely as friendly.

You will find that this strategy is very effective in raising your tip level so why not try it? Put in a modern-day context, it is obviously less threatening when a female Server touches a male diner, however, this is not exclusively so. Either way, touching is a very effective technique that can be used to the extent of your own comfort level.

MIRROR IMAGING

Mirror imaging, or 'mimicry', has long been known as a body language technique for allowing people to become more relaxed. By copying their sub-conscious body language signs, particularly in tense situations such as interviews and inter-rogations, the questioner can calm or relax a person without them realizing what is being achieved.

Brought into a restaurant scenario, a recent study at the University of Nijmegen in Holland, has shown that Servers who copied their customers' behaviour received substantial-ly higher tips than those who didn't. Rick van Baaren of the University states of the diner:

"Mimicry creates bonds between people. It induces a sense of 'we-ness'. You know that what you're doing is okay and you become more generous (with the tip)."

Not only that but in what the University termed *"verbal mimicry"*, where Servers repeated customers' orders back to them, their average tip <u>doubled</u>! – and this is in a Country where service charges are included in all restaurant bills.

again, simple, yet dramatic.

y opinion, the repeating of orders back to the diners su. ild happen on every occasion as, not only does this reduce the opportunity for mistakes, it also gives you, the Server, added opportunities for eye-contact, verbal bonding and showing the diners that their personal menu choices are important to you and being accepted.

In addition, similar studies concluded that "smiling, greeting and touching the customer (see 'Touching' above) and crouching down beside them while taking orders (see 'The Bends' below) also lead to bigger tips."

I encourage you to study this report as it could affect you greatly.

THE BENDS

No, not the affliction that deep-sea divers suffer when they surface too quickly from the deep but the affliction some Servers have when they talk with their seated customers.

As a diner, I find it very annoying, while seated, to have a Server towering over me, then bending at the waist so that his head lowers itself to communicate with me. This position of superiority does nothing for me – just bugs the heck out of me. I don't like talking to a person whose head is sideways to me, whose eyes I find difficulty in engaging and a person who is trying to communicate in quite an unnatural position.

As mentioned above, mimicry has very definite advantages and squatting is just a form of mimicking your diners' seated posture. Even drawing up a spare chair, if available and the circumstances warrant, will achieve the friendly outcome you are seeking. If you come down to their level, the superiority card will not be an issue and your diners will feel more comfortable. Your eye contact will be more direct and your diners will feel less threatened by your close proximity, if that would normally be an issue with them.

These studies can't all be wrong. This is highly touted as a definite tip increaser. I know it's very acceptable for me, as a diner.

THE SMILE

The power of the smile can never be overstated.

Back in ancient times the human smile meant, *"Look. I'm a friend. You can see I have no teeth with which I can tear you apart."*

These days, a smile is just a friendly welcome. It's very difficult when a person smiles at another for that other person not to smile back. It's infectious, creates a lighter heart and initiates friendly conversation in people that might, otherwise, just pass each other by.

I think, perhaps, that our modern-day culture may be to blame for it to be so difficult to smile, these days.

"We can't show our emotions."

"We can't trust strangers, therefore we can't smile at them."

"We can't talk to them. We don't know them."

Some even feel it to be a sign of weakness. Can you imagine that? A restaurant should be a fun place full of satisfied diners and happy Servers.

Happy Servers? Now there's a concept. You are happy at your work, aren't you?

It is a universally accepted concept that if you put a smile on your face just before you answer a ringing phone then your mood will be perceived to be happy by the caller, regardless of how you felt before picking up the phone.

Why not try it in the seclusion and privacy of your own home, first. Just smile and feel your mood change up a few gears. When the phone rings, put a smile on your face before answering it. I'll wager that your attitude is different than if you just picked up the receiver and said "allo" or "Yeah". I guarantee that it will work every single time.

As a diner, I like to see a Server who is quick to smile, not necessarily with a stupid smile on their face all the time – that would be unreasonable. Quick to smile, yet immediately responsive to all diners is very effective strategy and the mood is always catching. Show them that you actually do enjoy serving them. That effect will not go unnoticed and don't be put off by their sometime unsmiling countenances. Plan to win them over before their entrees are placed in front of them.

To go with your smile, do you have a 'joke-of-the-day' perhaps? Most times, jokes can be perfect 'ice-breakers', particularly if they are self-deprecating, that is about Servers or restaurants. The internet is full of such sites and as long as you don't use the same one in the hearing of a table you've already told it to, you won't need more than two or three jokes for the whole day!

Being in a restaurant that is charged with such positive energy is very infectious and when it infects your diners – how could your tips diminish?

If you can embrace these variations of body language concepts in your daily work, you will very soon experience the fact that:

Copycat Servers get bigger tips

HERMAN®

11-23

**"Grab your shepherd's pie.
It's fourth from the top."**

The Server

THE SECOND MOST IMPORTANT PERSON IN THE HOUSE

Before discussing how you can better serve your customers let us understand exactly what it is that motivates you to serve and the customers to dine.

Firstly, why is it that men and women, girls and boys become Servers? What's the main purpose for doing this hard, sometimes thankless, work?

Now, it's true that the vast majority of you Servers thoroughly enjoy your work. Many part-time Servers enjoy the added freedom to pursue other work interests, schooling or just relaxing at home. The work may perfectly suit your intellectual needs: no two days the same, a highly social environment, continually meeting new people in a non-threatening environment, fast moving yet relaxed atmosphere – at least relaxed-looking on the public side, but that's another story!

However, the main purpose of doing what you do is more basic:

THE MAIN PURPOSE YOU DO WHAT YOU DO IS TO EARN MONEY!

Money. – the most basic of substances that, in this society, allows you to do so much more with your life. The more you have, the more you can do. It's that simple. I have yet to meet a Server who works purely for the love of the work itself without interest or regard for money earned.

Although this may sound harsh, it's true. When I first considered this project, I didn't want to present this theory just as my opinion so I created a short questionnaire on the topic and distributed it to as many dining establishments as I could in a two-month period. As you can see from the results in the separate chapter *'Server Questionnaire'*, money is a very powerful motivator for the vast majority of Servers who responded.

I don't want to become too bogged down by statistics in this book. However, the questionnaire is reproduced here, with a summary of the results in the chapter entitled *'Server Questionnaire'*. (Page 95)

I think you can see that the overwhelming driving force is the necessity of earning as much money as possible and, to this end, the main thread running through this book and repeated often is:

How to hone your serving and communication skills to increase your overall income.

If this financial increase comes from your customers in higher-percentage gratuities then it automatically follows that they are more satisfied with their time with you and reflect that by giving you more money. Remember, gratuities are, for the most part, voluntary so an increase in gratuity percentage shows a corresponding increase in serving quality, in the customers' perception , page 95

Personally, as a diner, I like this freedom to appreciate good work by a Server and, as mentioned before, will not willingly frequent those establishments where a mandatory gratuity is added.

Again, ask yourself whether the desire to earn money is your main reason for being employed there. You provide a service for which you should receive as much remuneration as you possible can. We all know that, in Server positions, the hourly rate is usually very basic, so you have a prime interest in receiving as high a gratuity as possible to supplement your basic earnings.

Even if you are in a position of pooling your gratuities, your interests are the same. Only now, you should be keen to see that <u>all</u> Servers, in your establishment, try to maximize the tips at their tables as well. Teamwork is a valuable concept in the serving industry.

There are a number of different factors that influence the amount of money you can earn, some of which are directly under your control, some controlled by Management and some which can be influenced by effective team work, particularly where gratuity pooling is concerned.

Most importantly, the factors under your direct control include:

1. Your personality and customer service ability

2. Direct communication skills

3. Physical appearance and cleanliness

4. Menu, beverage and wine list knowledge

5. Work availability

6. Professionalism

7. Body language skills

8. Speaking and listening skills

Factors controlled by Management include:

1. Management relationship with server

2. Management operational skills

3. Fairness with wage rate

4. Fairness with scheduling

5. Fairness with gratuity pool sharing

6. Team training

Factors influenced by effective team work include:

1. High efficiency team approach to customer service

2. Concerted effort to maximize the gratuity pool

3. Ensure that all team members understand the common goals

4. Ability to present, discuss and implement fresh ideas to Management

5. Encourage less-able team members to become more proficient

While some of these factors are beyond your control, most can be controlled and will materially affect your final income. What is considered 'good' and 'bad' service can change from country to country, region to region or even establishment to establishment and, therefore, is too big an issue to deal with here. Who is to say that throwing your steak bones on the floor is 'bad' when set in a mediaeval context? However, it is presumed that you know 'good' service from 'bad' in your working environment and understand the basic concept that the better service you can give, the more money you can expect to receive.

After all, it is the perception of the customer that counts. The customer is the one who pays the bill, decides on and awards the tip!

These days, there are many gimmicks applied to increase customer expenditure: theme restaurants, Servers dressed as monks, Servers dressed as tarts, Servers dressed all in black or, in one location I know, Servers dressed in nothing at all! Sung birthday greetings with a complimentary slice of cake is popular as are dancing bartenders – the variations seem never-ending. Don't forget that only those gimmicks that tend to increase gratuities have an immediate and direct effect on your own income. In other words, if a customer suggests that it would not be a good idea to celebrate their birthday with an embarrassing group singing 'Happy Birthday' at the table then it would be a good idea to shelve that gimmick at that table, on that occasion. In my opinion, nothing increases gratuities like good, honest personal communication, particularly with the person who will be paying the bill.

What is your job as a Server?

In the nicest way possible, it is your job to encourage the customers to pay as much money as possible while they are there, not just by ordering an entrée but by up-selling them with cocktails, hors d'ouvres, wine, dessert, coffees, liqueurs, etc. As mentioned previously, take care that this up-selling does not impede a good table turn-round rate in busy periods. If you've done your job well and to the satisfaction of the customers, a healthy gratuity will follow and your job satisfaction will be high.

GREETING

The original greeting to your customer, on entering your restaurant, is most important but, generally, not under your control. Your Reception Team has one chance to make a good first impression and if they blow it, the pressure's on. If you are aware that the 'front end' has already been a little stressful for your customers before they reach your table, it would be wise to show concern for them for their wait time, a drafty waiting area, the lack of crayons for the kids, etc. and always end up with:

"... but I'm glad you're here with me now."

Like it or not, as a Server, whether for breakfast, lunch or dinner, one of your main tasks is as a stress reliever to your customers. You must, therefore, always be prepared to empathize with your customers and listen to their concerns, rather than side with your Reception Team. The Reception Team will not be serving your customers for the next hour or awarding you your gratuity!

Your initial greeting with your customer(s) is most important and can set the scene for their whole dining experience. If you know their names, either by their reservation record or by the wait-list, then you should address them by their names often. This will help to personalize the relationship, giving them a feeling of importance and connection with you.

Consider these vitals actions as essential in every first customer greeting of your Serving life:

1. Your smile should be all over your face before you first gain eye-contact

2. The fact that you're genuinely pleased to see them should be their first impression of you

3. Your cheery greeting should include your name right up front. Not *"Hi. My name's Amy and I'll be your server today"*. I think everyone sees through that one! It should be more on the lines of *"Hi. I'm Amy. Welcome to *** (name of restaurant)."* Other phrases such as *"I'm really pleased to be looking after you this evening."* And *"What terrible weather outside but we're warm and dry in here."* or any other suitable phrase can be added as you think fit, depending on your own initial assessment of them. The old phrase that 'you never get a second chance to make a first impression' is never truer than in these circumstances. Always maximize your chance to personalize your initial greeting with them right from your first sentence and remember those open-ended questions.

4. Always allow them to settle in their seats at their own speed. If they feel they are being rushed, at this stage, it will be that much harder for you to achieve an on-going friendly, relaxed atmosphere.

This has nothing to do with Servers and increasing gratuities but...

I do remember walking into a restaurant in Nashville, Tennessee, one rainy, Winter's evening and right into a wait time of 45 minutes. Initially, of course, I was frustrated but decided to wait as the alternative of finding another restaurant, without a wait time, was too daunting.

About five minutes into my wait, with about 12 other would-be patrons, in the lobby area, a young man, about 16 years old, appeared and started to do simple card tricks for us. For the three waiting young kids, he produced a seemingly endless supply of Hershey's Kisses from their ears. It appears that he was the Manager's son, had done his school homework and just wanted to practice his hobby.

We were all thoroughly diverted from the long wait, enjoyed the performance and, probably more importantly, the three kids were so absorbed that they were quiet and we were all 'whine' and 'wriggle-free' for the whole waiting time. In addition, all the waiting customers stayed and not one of them left in frustration.

I have no idea whether this contravened any entertainment license requirements, or not. It was simple genius, in my mind and I'd certainly go back, if only to find out where those confounded Hersheys kept coming from!

It was a great evening, all round.

My guess is that little diversion didn't harm the Server's' gratuities one little bit, either!

I remember my first serving position as a flight attendant with British Airways – just a restaurant in the sky, really. The essence of our work was not primarily to please the passengers but to ensure that they flew with us on subsequent occasions. The rationale was that if we achieved the latter, the former would look after itself. As I'm sure you know, no tips were involved in that job. However, job security was a major incentive and returning passengers helped achieve such security – much like returning restaurant patrons, I guess.

At first blush, you may only see a subtle distinction between the two concepts of satisfying your customers in the moment or satisfying your customers so that they are encouraged to return. However, you'll find that if you communicate with the prospect of seeing your customers again on subsequent visits they will feel more important, more comfortable and more relaxed. This should not just be in your final farewell –

"... and I look forward to seeing you again soon"

but during their time with you with such comments as

"Yes, I can see your dilemma between the two entrees. Our tenderloin has been very well received, this evening, so might I suggest that you order our pork now and our prime rib, which is always excellent, perhaps you can try on your next visit with us?"

or

"As you can see from our menu, we have some superb daily specials. Our salmon, today, is excellent. May I also mention that Sunday's all-you-can-eat roast beef dinner is great value and well worth returning for."

This type of communication will help to create a bond with your customers, intimating that there is more to be enjoyed in the future and insinuate into their sub-conscious that your establishment is worth subsequent, if not frequent, visits.

Never say, *"Can I take your order?"*, *"Ready to order?"* or *"What do you want?"* By asking any of these types of questions you are setting up a master/servant relationship with no warmth and definitely not a friendly, welcoming one.

Remember, You are a Server – not a servant!

Ask yourself this very important question. Who ever tips a servant? Try questions like:

- *"Have you decided on your entrée?"*
- *"Can I help you with our menu choices?"*
- *"Would you prefer a few more minutes? There's no rush."*

If you are able to take their orders without writing them down, so much the better as this helps to maintain a more informal atmosphere. However, if you do have to use an order pad then don't hide behind it. Write only when they have stopped talking and keep it brief. You might like to create a code so that the time taken in writing will be minimal.

Regardless of whether you have to write orders down or not,

Always, always, always repeat back to each diner, the menu choices they've made.

I know we've dealt with this previously. However, I believe that it's so important that it is well worth repeating. Not only will repeating the order to the diner reduce the opportunity for error, it will reinforce the diner's personal selection to themselves and also encourages a greater anticipation of what they'll later receive.

When a Server repeats my selection to me <u>I know</u> I'm dealing with a professional.

How many times has a customer asked, *"What's good today?"* – as if you'll tell them what's bad today! What a stupid question. Anyway, dumb as it is, the *"What's good today?"* question offers an ideal time for you to suggest the more popular dishes served so far, adding some recent customer comments for added 'flavour', topped off with your personal recommendation. Don't forget, for that moment, you are their expert and their advisor.

You can also take this opportunity to get to know them better by asking them questions. It's no good telling them that the salmon is *"good today"* if they don't eat seafood. Once you have determined what kind of food they are looking for and you are able to recommend one or two items from your menu, this might also be the occasion to relate their likes to your taste.

Don't be tempted to just say,

"Yes, that's a favourite tonight."

but elaborate, maybe with the following,

"That's one of <u>my</u> favourites, too, mainly because of <u>our</u> chef's cheese and red wine sauce, which really is to die for."

By discussing their choices in this manner, not only are you bonding with them with your mutual likes, you are creating an expectancy in their minds for their meal to come. This expectancy is very important as it bonds the diner to their personal choice of meal and raises the level of positive energy at their table. If you believe that your *thoughts create your reality* then if the diner is waiting for 'fish and chips' then all he will receive will be

"fish and chips"

Pretty 'blah'. If, on the other hand, your diner has been primed to expect:

"two filets of fresh halibut, prepared in <u>our</u> chef's own beer batter then served with home-style seasoned French fries and cole slaw, freshly made on <u>our</u> premises daily',

Then that is what will be in his mind while his meal is being prepared right up until you return to his table and present it. In essence, you are conditioning your diner to believe that he/she is receiving something very special from you.

As mentioned before, in all communications with your diners, there is always a great tendency to use the word *'the'* instead of the personal pronoun *'your'* or *'my'* or *'our'* or *'I'* (underlined throughout this book). These personal pronouns are very powerful words and, together with strong adjectives or descriptive words, tend to increase your personal connection both with the food and with your diners in your conversations. Whenever you catch yourself saying the word 'the' when talking to your diners about *your* food or *your* restaurant you have lost an opportunity of bonding the customer into the personal relationship that you are trying to achieve.

Maybe your dining establishment should incorporate a fine box for every time the word "The" is used.

Think of it this way:

'THE'

is a dull, neutral word, totally devoid of any personality, pizzazz, character or sizzle.

Not the best word to rely on for a big fat tip!

It is, therefore, very advantageous for the customer to feel a personal connection as soon as possible, particularly at the ordering stage. Their personal choice has been made and it is good. As soon as customers feel ownership to their choice, or that of their companion(s) they will often be quite defensive about it, even to the point of failing to comment on any minor deficiencies with it; underdone, small portion, etc. that may subsequently come up:

Instead of saying:	*"The steak is good"*
Try:	*"Our New York steak is simply excellent, tonight"*
Instead of saying:	*"The house wine is a Merlot"*
Try:	*"Our house wine tonight is a Californian Merlot, chosen by our chef for its full-bodied, rich flavour. May I bring you a small sample?"*

Instead of saying:	*"Try the fish"*
Try:	*"<u>My</u> favourite is <u>our</u> poached salmon. It always looks delicious and has been very popular with <u>our</u> customers tonight."*
Instead of saying:	*"The Cheesecake?"*
Try:	*"<u>Our</u> Grand Marnier cheesecake is to die for. Perhaps <u>you</u>'d like to share one on this occasion? <u>I'll</u> be happy to bring <u>you</u> an extra fork?"*

These are just a few examples but I'm sure you can see how, with the addition of personal pronouns, these sentences have changed into much stronger and more friendly communications.

In addition, by using the word *"tonight"* or *"today"* or *"on this occasion"* you will bring a sense of immediacy to the specific item and this will tend to make the item more special to the occasion.

Don't be afraid of sprinkling in a few descriptive adjectives as well. *'Delicious'*, *'attractive'*, *'full-bodied'* are all words that make the hungry and thirsty salivate with anticipation.

For the diner, after all, it is all about the build-up of anticipation and the satisfaction that all five senses receive. Now it's true that not every diner is consciously aware of this scenario but you will certainly hear of it if one of their senses is let down. *"This tastes awful" "This smells off" "That oyster didn't quite taste right. Where's the washroom?"* I think you get my drift.

Of course, not every meal is perfect and not every occasion ends without incident. However, if you've cemented a strong personal bond with your customers, right from the beginning, you'll find that <u>they will team up with you</u> to resolve whatever problems arise. If they see you to be on 'their side' their gratitude will not waiver when the final bill is to be paid.

The balance you are trying to achieve is one of helpful friendliness without being subservient or too deferential.

You will know when you find this balance as you will feel a comfortable measure of partnership with your diners and a freedom to make suggestions, discuss timing, offer alternate choices, etc.

A good server can overcome shortcomings in the kitchen much better than a chef can overcome lousy service at the tables.

There have been many studies on the effect of giving candies to diners at the end of their meals and not one of them suggested that tips were negatively affected when candies were given. On the contrary, the higher quality of candy given seemed to directly increase the amount of tips. I won't blind you with the many statistics on this topic but it's clear that if your employer does not supply candies then it would be well worth your while to buy them yourself for your customers. Although mints are a better aid to digestion, miniature wrapped chocolates are more highly favoured, as they are conceived as a more valuable luxury gift.

I have already discussed the concept of lightly touching your customer on the shoulder as you present the bill to make this part of the meal more friendly. Well, you should also consider re-emphasizing your name that you gave them, right at the first meeting, by writing it on the bill – not on the back of the bill but on the front where their financial obligations have been itemized. You can also draw a personal design on the bill as well. You don't have to be a Rembrandt to create this as it only needs to be a happy scribble. If you'd like to go to the extra effort of creating your own-designed rubber (preferably self-inking) stamp with your own *'smiley face'*, *'sunshine'*, *'stick person'* or whatever suits your personality, with the word *'Thanks'* prominently displayed, now that would be very effective.

I guarantee that the bill-payer's final thoughts before awarding your gratuity will be of you.

This very personal touch is your last opportunity to positively affect your customer in his/her decision on the outcome of your tip. It is very simple, yet very effective.

Finally, remember:

If you can't influence your wages
Then influence your tips!

HERMAN®

5-12

70

How's Everything?

THAT DREADED QUESTION

The hard work has been done.
  You have already:

- Personally greeted your customers and established a relationship,

- Arranged their seating,

- Taken their coats,

- Poured each one their glass of iced water,

- Taken their beverage order and served them their drinks,

- Advised on starter selections,

- Guided them through their personal menu choices,

- Suggested suitable wines for their menu choices,

- Presented their hors d'ouvres,

- Poured their selected wines,

- Served each one their entrees,

- Topped up their wine glasses, and

- Generally looked after their every need.

So far – since their arrival – you've created a unique personal relationship where your customers have come to rely on you and your skills for a good, relaxed dining experience. The ambience is good. You've created a high level of anticipation for both food and drink and now you've satisfied that anticipation with service of the various entrees.

You are satisfied with everything. You have your customers comfortable and looking to you for all their needs. As we agreed earlier, your main purpose in being a Server is to maximize your income and you can certainly look forward to a good tip from this friendly table, under these circumstances.

Make no mistake about it. It is you who have created this goodwill by your personality and your serving skills. You are convincing them that they have chosen well by coming to your establishment and will be very pleased that they are at *your* table. Almost like family.

Feel good?

You deserve to.

Then you return to their table and ask the most inane, stupid, de-personalizing, mindless, destructive and unanswerable of all questions:

"HOW'S EVERYTHING?"

Now, I know you have been instructed by Management to ask this de-personalizing question of each table, once entrees have been served or you say it purely out of habit because everyone else says it.

Crazy!

72

As discussed earlier, every utterance of that question is a significant lost opportunity for added personal income.

Think about it –

Each item in the list that started this chapter contains personal actions:

- *Personally* making each one of them comfortable

- Advising each patron on their *personal* food selections

- Suggesting the perfect wine for their *personal* preference

- You have taken care and energy *personalizing* their respective meals with choices they have made for a comfortable dining experience.

- You may even have skillfully guided them to a second *personal* entrée choice, if their first selection was not available.

- Maybe, they even made a *personal* choice on the type of dinner rolls you presented.

Then you return to the table. Forgetting that your prime purpose is to maximize your income by encouraging a large gratuity, <u>you immediately de-personalize the whole preceding process</u> by asking that incredible mind-numbing of all questions:

"How's Everything?"

By asking that single general question you are attempting to cover the personal choices and decisions of everyone at the table in a three-second interruption. Yes, interruption it is, for you cannot hope to continue your very friendly personal approach with a question like that. Most Servers I've come across seem content to mindlessly 'shoot themselves in the foot' at this stage, merely to expect a response of *"fine"* then to leave the table, dismissed as quickly as the question was asked.

Do you get the impression that this question steams my cookies to boiling point?

By your thoughtless actions, this customer interaction just becomes a mere ritual:

- You ask the question,

- The response of *"fine"*, *"excellent"* or even *"okay"* is fired back and then,

- You retreat, maybe wondering why all that positive, friendly positive energy suddenly evaporated.

In mindlessly (there's that word 'mindless' again) performing this ritual, you have reduced all your good *personal* work to that of the mundane and taken an obviously huge backward step from the relationship previously created.

Do the patrons recognize this as a backward step?

Most probably not.

Maybe they don't even give it a thought. Consider this. They don't tick off a long questionnaire at the end of a dining experience before awarding a tip. When checking their bill, they probably give the service one brief conscious thought, then pick a percentage.

If you do not stand out then neither will your percentage.

Primarily – You failed to maintain the personal nature of the relationship by demeaning – yes, demeaning – their individual *personal* choices to the bland title *"everything"*. You will have de-personalized their service right at the pinnacle of their experience when anticipation of taste and smell meet – harmoniously we hope – with their actual experience. Now that is when you should be there, not de-personalizing their choices with *that question* but re-personalizing their experience with more intelligent and personal questions based, if you are able, on previous conversational comments. I have listed a few such questions below but, really, the list is endless as every relationship you have with your customers will be unique.

You have to ask yourself whether, by asking *that question*, you expect or want an intelligent answer? Are you asking for a detailed list of the merits or demerits of all food and drink consumed thus far? Is that what you mean by asking, *"How's everything?"* Of course not!

The real reason you should ask any questions is to maintain or heighten the personal relationship you have with the person who will later be awarding your tip. We have discussed before whether this is too selfish a concept but, don't forget, if you do receive a very large gratuity, it simply means the customer and his/her guests are highly satisfied with your service. Remember, no-one is going to pay you for doing a lousy job. Contrary to some beliefs, customers have no responsibility towards your basic income or your tip levels.

…but back to the plot!

The additional annoying factor is that the *"How's everything?"* question is often asked without any regard to the customers' ability to answer. By that, I mean that the Server will walk up to the table and ask *the dreaded question* immediately, without first checking to see whether the customer is eating or talking to other members of the group at the time and, therefore, unable to answer. I have often been asked *the dreaded question by* a Server who is passing by my table, with someone else's meals in their hands and not even stopping for an answer or even gaining eye-contact. I find that incredible. What a lost opportunity.

To give *superlative* customer service why can't my Server make a specific trip to my table and make a specific, intelligent and concerning enquiry of my satisfaction with my food, thus far?

This seems to happen so often to me and I find it baffling why a Server would sabotage their previously friendly actions by making me so frustrated. It's an indication to me that they just don't care. This is important as, after all, I will be paying the bill and the gratuity percentage will be my choice!

Before making any comment on a customers' entrée:

1. *First:*
   Ensure that they have actually tasted their entree so they can give you an informed comment.

2. *Next:*
   Make sure they are actually able to respond. That is they are not eating or in mid-conversation with each other.

3. *Finally:*
   Keep using personal pronouns and positive descriptive adjectives as suggested below.

This very important communication must remain part of your strategy to secure for yourself or your team the highest gratuity possible. Don't forget, as I mentioned before:

You are there for their benefit, not the other way round.

By asking the <u>right</u> questions you can acknowledge the time and effort the diner expended to make his/her *personal* choice. The diner will feel that you really do care, not only about the food they have chosen and you have just served but their *personal* enjoyment of the food as well.

You've promised and now you've delivered.

Instead of bleating out *"How's everything?"* you can say:

- *"Is <u>your</u> prime rib to <u>your</u> liking?"* or

- *"<u>Your</u> New York Strip looks so delicious. <u>I</u> think <u>I'll</u> join <u>you</u>."*

- *"Did <u>our</u> chef prepare <u>your</u> salmon as <u>you</u> requested?"*

- *"<u>I</u> mentioned to the chef that <u>you</u> liked <u>your</u> peppercorn sauce hot. Was <u>he</u> successful?"*

The variations are endless but the last two suggestions are the most powerful as they ask for the diner's opinion and he/she can't respond with just *"fine"*. As you know, whenever anyone is asked their personal opinion on anything, they feel appreciated and good in themselves. As mentioned earlier, if you can tie in your question with a previous conversation topic, then so much the better.

Always give this occasion some preparation so that your question is apt and benefits you. Once again, we come back to open-ended communication. If you can structure your question so that it begs an answer of more than one syllable like *"fine"*, *"good"*, *"okay"*, etc., the customer will consciously have to think of a suitable reply and this will reinforce in them the fact that you really care about their enjoyment. If they are subconsciously waiting for the *"How's everything?"* question they will be pleasantly surprised when you ask an intelligent question in place of the regular mundane ritual. It will jog their mind and most will respond with thought and intelligence.

Instead of thinking of this part of your job as a three-second interruption on your way to do something else, consider spending as much time at the table as is necessary to re-affirm your personal connection with your diners.

It is imperative that you ask your question initially to the person who will be paying – The *'leader'*, as we earlier discussed. The *'leader'* will appreciate the focus and his/her positive response may well set the tone for the rest of the group. I have yet to see one group member complain after the *'leader'* has commented on all being well.

After this, your options are open, either to address each of the group members individually to enquire about their personal entrees or collectively in general with, *"Is there anything else that I can now bring you?"* That will allow for any of the group to ask for any individual wants such as condiments, more water, bread, etc. You have now deferred to the *'leader'* and looked after his group members without reducing the personal aspect of your service.

Your body language will be different for each strategy. If you are addressing the *'leader'* then focus directly on that person with eye contact, direct body direction and lower vocal volume. If you're addressing the table group then your volume will be louder, your body will be more open with hands spread, as if to embrace the group and your eye contact will move from person to person. In most cases, the diners will not consciously be aware of your strategy but all will feel good about your personal attention.

Remember, when addressing a dining group with separate checks, the need to continue a personal relationship with each diner is paramount so you may wish to take a little extra time and enquire of each diner whether they're enjoying their entrée. This will be your choice and obviously dependant on the size of the group.

Keep working them, though. It'll be worth it.

Negative comments, however, do arise and it is essential that you handle such comments just as personally and just as professionally. Let them know that, whatever has occurred, you are on their side. Don't forget that your ambition is still to maximize your gratuity and diners always appreciate a swift resolution to any problem. It is, therefore, in your best interests to resolve all complaints without question and immediately. As we all know, the pleasure of dining out is to dine together. A substitute entrée or re-created entree, most times, causes difficulties for the group as delays are inevitably incurred. A group of two is highly susceptible to dissatisfaction when such delays occur.

This has happened rarely to me but I do remember one occasion where I had to send my entrée back.

I was dining with three others in a celebratory environment and our entrees were all served together. They looked excellent but my chicken was not good at all.

On mentioning this to our server she had the presence of mind to suggest that maybe a 'special' appetizer plate be served as a substitute so that any delay in re-presenting a suitable entrée be minimized. I accepted this excellent compromise and we all continued to eat together, with only a minimal delay for me.

I can still remember the server's exact words on that occasion. She truly understood the concept as she said, "The chicken I served you should not even have been brought into our kitchen in the first place. I will take it away immediately." She de-personalized my chicken by reverting to the 'The' word and the 'it' word then assumed full responsibility by saying "...I served you..." and finally made the whole problem disappear by saying "...I will take it away immediately." Did you catch all those personal pronouns? Very impressive.

I don't know whether this was just intuitive on her

part or she had been trained to follow that course. From my aspect, though, her actions couldn't have been more professional.

After we had dined and I received the bill I was pleased to see that she had not charged me for the 'appys' and I was happy to leave a gratuity much higher than it normally would have been. I understood that it wasn't the Server's fault that the entrée was well below par and I appreciated her initiative in keeping our group on course (excuse the pun) and happy. We had a great evening and our server maintained that personal service right up to an including the bill.

Oh… and yes. We have been back there a number of times, since.

During my research for this book I talked with many people on the topic and most of them said that they had not noticed any effect *that question* had on them at all. It was just too common an occurrence and was accepted, by them, as a 'means-nothing', everyday dining ritual that one puts up with to humour the Server. That's right, to humour the Server!

"How's everything?"
"Fine."

"How's everything?"
"Fine."

"How's everything?"
"Fine."

They were mostly unanimous of the fact that *the question* was invariably asked of them and dismissed by them just as quickly. They did concede, though, on deeper consideration, that the use of the *'dreaded question'* was a significant lost communication opportunity for a Server interested in trying to maximize their relationship with a diner.

Universally, though, they now curse me for ruining their dining-out experiences as, once their entrees arrive in front of them, they now <u>all</u> wait for that ritual dreaded question:

"HOW'S EVERYTHING?"

HERMAN®

by Jim Unger

"There's the bill and here's
a photo of my wife and kids."

Conclusion

THE TIP AT THE END OF THE MEAL

What's the difference between a book and a Server?

> *A book you can put down, pick up, put down, then pick up again and read all the pages over and over again.*
>
> *A Server, however, only has one chance to make a good first impression, one short time-frame to influence a good gratuity from a diner and with no re-run ability!*

That is why you should study and become comfortable with all the various techniques described here – and other places – to become more professional and more personal in your work. From the time you first greet your new customers you can then immediately look after their needs expertly and receive good money for that care.

I hope this short book has given you some insight into us, the diners of this World. What we think, what we need and, more importantly, what you can do to entice more money from our pockets to yours in the name of *superlative* customer service.

For those of you who are still doubters I know that you're not going to win us all.

While I've met my share of lousy Servers in my time, I'm the first to admit that there are many more rude, disrespectful, angry, finger-snapping, arrogant diners around. To grin and bear these diners <u>and</u> give them *superlative* service takes a lot of doing and your patience in dealing with those 'creeps' is highly commendable. However, even amongst the so-called 'ordinary' diners there will be those who will not tip, regardless of how well they are served. Disappointing though this is, it has to be remembered that there is no law that demands diners pay a tip (other than those restaurants where a fixed gratuity is written right up front on the menu and even that is just a civil contract, for the most part).

Let's review a few points here to put this point in perspective:

> *As with most occupations, being a Server is a voluntary occupation. Although you may feel that your job is crucial to you for the income it gives you, you can leave and look for something else if you become too frustrated or can't earn enough money.*
>
> *As an individual Server or as a collective group of Servers, do you really think you can change individual diners' tipping habits by any method, other than by superlative customer service?*
>
> *Has the 'icy stare', given to a cheap diner over a small or zero tip, ever resulted in you receiving a higher gratuity from that diner?*

There are times when, no matter how *superlative* your service, you will receive less than you're worth. These are the times when you should take a deep breath and deeply soul-search your own actions to see whether you could have done anything at all that would have increased your tip. If, on these occasions, you can think past your personal feelings of disappointment, maybe even anger and look objectively at your customer service style, you may be surprised to find areas where you could have performed better. It probably won't be just one thing. There may be a number of little actions that you could have bettered. These actions could have resulted in a closer relationship with the diner being forged and a consequent higher tip awarded.

This is not meant to sound patronizing but the plain fact is that a diner goes into an eating establishment to eat food that is priced clearly in the menu. <u>The diner has a basic expectation of good food and good service.</u> That's all. The rest <u>has</u> to be up to you.

In order to be generous, the paying diner has to be motivated into recognizing that he/she has received more than their basic expectations and this is where you come in with your *superlative* customer service.

Remember, you cannot demand a tip.
You have to earn a tip.

Recently, Lynnette and I revisited a regular' haunt' of ours, a medium-sized chain restaurant, and were surprised for the first time to receive superlative customer service.

As we were leaving, we sought out the Manager to compliment him on his staff and to identify two of them who were truly superlative. The Manager, obviously pleased with our positive comments, asked for particulars. We told him that we really enjoyed the personal nature of their service and the fact that they appeared to have read who we were and what we needed very well.

The Manager seemed concerned at this and said that

he tries to encourage his Servers <u>not</u> to be too personal with their customer approach. I then pointed out to him that he, The Manager, does not receive any part of the tips his Servers earn and, maybe, he should consider the more personal approach as it was very successful with my wife and I and resulted in a 25% tip to the waiter. We also pointed out that we were also very keen to revisit his restaurant on our next visit to town.

Now, we continued talking with the Manager for some time, after this but I don't know whether I made any impression on him at the end of it. I guess I have to recognize that, in this social climate, in some large restaurant chains, there may be safety in 'dumbing down' the service angle so that a set style can be taught that, they believe, will also minimize the risk of customer complaints.

The direct result of this strategy is to reduce the opportunity for increasing your tips so I feel you should make your own decision as to what is important to you and what strategy to follow.

Odd to think that I may even have contributed to the disciplining of the two Servers by their Manager for commending their high service level. Weird.

Good customer service is insufficient these days to achieve a significant increase in tips. It must be *superlative customer service...* and it must be consistent. If you are able to slip into the habit of continually trying to upgrade your service, you will achieve this aim and, as a bi-product, receive much higher job satisfaction by the mere fact that you'll be that much more successful.

It really is that easy. Feel free to put this book down, pick it up again and re-read it from cover to cover. You can do it. It can only help.

Now, I can hear some of you doubters say that this is a lot of

HERMAN®

"If you only want to spend twenty dollars, I'd recommend two hamburgers and a six-dollar tip."

effort, too much of that thinking stuff and there's no guarantee of more money at the end of it. Well, you're right on one point – there is no guarantee of more money at the end of it. All I can say is that it's up to you. If you change nothing then absolutely nothing will change and you'll be proved right!

On this topic, Geoff Lieberman of SYSCO, Seattle once made this very important statement:

> *"Insanity is duplicating the same behaviour repeatedly and expecting a different result."*

Quite simply, I believe that:

> *"Insanity is not trying to increase your income!"*

As mentioned before, it doesn't really matter what type of establishment you are working in – the principles are the same. All customers like to feel important and cared for and, if you adapt what you've read here to your particular workplace, I know you will succeed in becoming wealthier.

> *I recall reading an article by a self-described "career waiter" who insisted on keeping himself and the identity of his restaurant a secret.*
>
> *This Server's sole focus seemed to be the criticism of diners who don't declare their need for separate checks when they enter his restaurant, diners who spend a long time at dinner without over-tipping and diners who still think a 10% tip is fine. He even complained about diners who paid him verbal compliments instead of increasing his tip.*
>
> *At no time, in that article, did he acknowledge any responsibility for actually earning his tip. In fact, I doubt whether he fully understood the concept of why he should give diners any customer service at all!*

I know that it's easy to say,

> *"No matter what I do, the result will always be the*
> *same. They won't tip."*

I've come across this attitude often. However, if your customers speak your language or you can make yourself understood then you have the ability to change their attitude if you can just find a way to understand them a little better. If you can interpret their body language correctly and relate to them with this understanding then communicate with them more personally, using lots of *"I's"*, *"We's"*, *"You's"* and *"Our's"* you <u>will</u> change their perception of you. You <u>will</u> make a difference to them and they <u>will</u> increase their tips to you.

What skills do you need to achieve this income increase?

First of all:

> You must have a keen desire to become better at what you do. No one can expect to receive extra money when no extra effort has been expended.

Next:

> You must have the ability to be self-critical – not so much in a negative way but in a self-improving way. To achieve a higher income, you will constantly need to adjust your customer service style until you reach the *superlative* level and, unless you work for a very enlightened ownership/management, you'll have to do it all yourself.

Lastly:

> You must have patience. You may be able to grasp these concepts, put them into effect straight away and realize immediate results. However, for most, it will take

a little time. For most, by progressively changing your style, 'reading' your diners and adapting to each to suit their needs, you will see an increase in your tip-income steadily happening.

The art of understanding human nature is not that difficult to master. In your establishment, it will be a blend of good listening skills, keen observation of body language signals and constant questioning of yourself on understanding your customers' actual needs. We have covered this already but it bears repeating that, if you ask yourself the following questions each time you meet new customers, your understanding of them will increase considerably:

- ***Who are they?***

- ***Who will be paying?***

- ***Why are they here?***

- ***Where are they from?***

- ***What are their needs?***

Empathy is also a skill that should be one of your building blocks to excellence. Your customers will exhibit many characteristics that may tend to interrupt your normal working style and these include being old, slow, nervous, loud, brash, etc. None of these attributes will be directed personally against you and it will be to your advantage to understand the types of people you are dealing with. Work with, not against, their personal characteristics. After all, you're not going to be with them forever – just long enough to give them *superlative* service, planned to culminate in a generous tip when the final bill is paid. That is your main objective, isn't it?

Common sense is a little more difficult to define as it means different things to different people. However, within your own

HERMAN®

11-15   © Jim Unger/dist. by United Media, 2002

**"I just got fired, so I'll wait for
my tip outside the front door!"**

working environment, common sense will be closely related to the style of your eating establishment and the character of your diners. This is where 'reading' your customer is most important as it will be what your customer accepts that controls your tip level.

This World is dynamic and whether we like it not everything and every person in it is in a constant state of change. However, if you decide to stick in the *"Coffee?"* groove then you should just be content with the small amounts of loose change you will earn as tips.

If you'd like to increase your income dramatically, then consider what is written here as a sort of launching pad on the topic. *'How's Everything'* only scratches the surface but it does expose a huge potential for all you Servers to dramatically increase your income.

Again, as a diner, I would like to encourage you all to search the internet, read the blogs and study all the reports you can find on the topics of additional income potential in the food service industry. Don't just restrict yourselves to the books written 'by the trade, for the trade'; see what others have to offer. Gain more knowledge of the very important topic of *'body language'*. Study the more readable books on human behaviour – not the intricate scientific papers but those books written for the 'laymen' such as *'The Naked Ape'* and *'The Human Zoo'*, both by Dr. Desmond Morris. These books will give you an excellent idea just where we, as human beings, have come from in our thinking and how easy our needs are to comprehend, if we just understand our origins a little more.

I have not come across one study yet that concludes that significant increases in tips cannot be achieved.

Finally:

> For an investment of a mere few hours your financial benefits can be dramatically increased,
>
> *I guarantee*
>
> and, as a frequent diner, passionately interested in creating *superlative* Servers and being served by them on every occasion,
>
> *I know.*

P.S.

A comment to those of you who are not in the serving profession and who dine out regularly:

Be patient when you hear the *"How's everything?"* question. I know, at the moment, it'll be a part of your dining experience on 95% of those dining-out occasions. However, as this figure reduces and Servers create more enlightened ways of serving you'd better, reward them generously for they will have made your dining experiences much more pleasurable.

BONNE APPETITE!

HERMAN®

5-21

© Jim Unger/dist. by United Media, 1998

"Any other complaints?"

Server Questionnaire

WHAT ARE YOUR NEEDS?

In an effort to find out the true motivations of Servers I distributed the following small survey to a mixture of different eating establishments, both in Canada and the States, with a request that the survey be completed and returned to me.

I encouraged anonymity, if needed, to promote as many responses as possible. From a total of four hundred questionnaires distributed, I received 247 responses, with the majority requesting anonymity. This, alone, raises certain concerns about their feelings of security. However, those questions are for another time.

I am very grateful for those who did reply. However, due to the relatively undocumented nature of the study this should not be considered a truly scientific result but merely a 'straw poll' that tends to show general results of what is important to the Server respondents.

I have added percentage totals in brackets against each question in the Survey.

Notes:

1. Answers to the first three questions clearly demonstrate the importance that money holds to the Servers in this profession.

2. The answers to question four tend to show that only a minority of Servers are actively trying to increase their tips. This may be due to ambivalence but also maybe a lack of knowledge that this book may help to resolve.

3. In my opinion, biased though it may be, the answers to question five show an insecurity in Servers who believe that if they can receive an 10% - 20% fixed gratuity, it would at least give them a security of income – though they wouldn't have to necessarily 'earn' it with *superlative* customer service. It was heartening, though, to see option c) as the predominant thought.

4. Question six answers showed a greater percentage of Servers wishing for full-time work from which it can be deduced that extra money would be very welcome indeed.

5. There were many varied comments in the 'Other' columns, some showing frustration, some humorous and some unprintable but none that help us with the main question of the importance of increasing income in this profession.

SERVER QUESTIONNAIRE

This questionnaire has been devised to research why you do what you do. Being in the frontline of the restaurant business, with the most direct customer contact, your professionalism and work ethic are most important and the results of this questionnaire will help to better identify the desires and motivations of your group.

This questionnaire has been designed for maximum confidentiality with no obligation to divulge any personal details, locations assigned or hours worked. Please answer all questions to the best of your ability by circling the correct answer or answers if more than one answer is appropriate.

Thank you:

1. Why do you work as a server?
    a) For the money   (81%)
    b) For the prestige   (8%)
    c) To meet people   (7%)
    d) To look after people   (1%)
    e) Other (please specify)   (3%)
    Other _____

2. Why is the money important to you?
    a) My only source of income   (58%)
    b) Need to pay for school   (23%)
    c) Helps to pay for luxuries   (12%)
    d) The money is not important to me   (5%)
    e) Other (please specify)   (2%)
    Other _____

3. How important are gratuities in your work?
    a) Essential – I couldn't survive without them (77%)

b)   Great – but my basic income is sufficient for me   (6%)

c)   Okay – They help to pay for the extras   (11%)

d)   Whatever!   (3%)

e)   Other (please specify)   (3%)

Other _____

4.   Do you consciously work to increase your gratuity from each customer?

a)   Yes – The better my service, the higher the
     tip, usually   (18%)

b)   Yes – It helps us all in the long run   (17%)

c)   No – The tips work out the same, anyway   (58%)

d)   No – It's not important to me   (5%)

e)   Other (please specify)   (2%)

Other _____

5.   Do you consider gratuities to be a Server's right or should they be earned?

a)   They should be 15% – 20% fixed percentage
     of the final bill   (18%)

b)   They should be 10% – 15% fixed percentage
     of the final bill   (10%)

c)   Gratuities should be optional, subject to
     customer service level   (68%)

d)   Gratuities should not be allowed or encouraged   (0%)

e)   Other (please specify)   (4%)

Other _____

6.   Describe the type of hours worked
     (If you wish to remain anonymous and you feel this question may identify you, please refrain from answering)

a)   Full-time   (22%)

b)   Part-time by choice due to school commitments   (22%)

c)   Part-time by choice due to domestic
     responsibilities   (12%)

d)   Part- time due to no full-time hours available   (35%)

e)   Other (please specify)   (9%)

Other _____

Many thanks for completing this quick questionnaire. Your assistance is very much appreciated.

HERMAN®

by Jim Unger

9-21

© Jim Unger/dist. by United Media, 2000

"Too spicy?"

Quips & Quotes

WORTH A SECOND LOOK

In no particular order, I have recreated, below, a selection of important quotes from the book that will help to focus your mind on what's important when considering how to increase your income.

	Quote	Chapter
1.	Copycat Servers get bigger tips	*Body Language*
2.	A good Server can overcome shortcomings in the kitchen much better than a chef can overcome lousy service at the tables	*The Server*
3.	Remember, if you can't influence your wages then influence your tips	*The Server*
4.	'THE' is a dull, neutral word, totally devoid of any pizzazz, character or sizzle	*The Server*
5.	The main purpose you do what you do is to earn money	*The Server*

6.	If you do not stand out then neither will your percentage	*How's Everything*
7.	Good customer service is insufficient these days…	*How's Everything*
8.	You are there for your diners' benefit – not the other way round	*The Customer*
9.	If you only pick up what is said aloud, you are missing half the message	*Body Language*
10.	Every look tells us what goes on inside the person who gives it	*Body Language*
11.	Hold their eyes. Smile. Who could resist?	*Body Language*
12.	It is a commonly held theory that if you touch a person you intensify the message you are giving by 300%.	*Body Language*
13.	Mimicry creates bonds between people	*Body Language*
14.	Where Servers repeated customers' orders back to them verbally, their average tip doubled!	*Body Language*
15.	The power of your smile can never be overstated	*Body Language*
16.	Happy Servers. Now there's a concept. You are happy at your work, aren't you?	*Body Language*
17.	Try it in the seclusion and privacy of your own home, first!	*Body Language*

18. You are a Server – not a servant.   *The Server*
    Who ever tips a servant?

19. Pun intended, your diners are your   *The Customer*
    'bread and butter'...

20. Life is lived in your restaurant   *The Customer*

21. The one who pays, most often,   *The Customer*
    is the one who tips

22. It is the 'leader' who controls the meal   *The Customer*

23. All it requires is *superlative*   *The Customer*
    Customer Service!

24. I usually just vote with my feet   *Introduction*

25. Never underestimate yourself.   *Introduction*
    Your job is crucial.

26. That was a lost income opportunity,   *Introduction*
    on the Server's part of receiving at
    least $10.50 more – and that's just
    from one table!

27. The customer is the most important   *Introduction*
    person in a restaurant

28. The Server is the second-most   *Introduction*
    important person in a restaurant

29. Anything at all that will increase your   *Introduction*
    customers' satisfaction will be
    welcomed by all

30. "Please do not tip me. I don't want   *Introduction*
    the money. give any extra cash I earn
    to someone else."

31. Never underestimate yourself.   *Introduction*
    Your job is crucial

32. Become an ex *"How's everything?"*   *How's Everything*
    Server
33. Resist the *"How's everything?"*   *How's Everything*
    addiction at all times
34. Strike the words from your memory!   *First Page*
35. You can gain the ability to   *How's Everything*
    <u>immediately</u> earn significantly
    more money
36. What does this customer really want?   *Introduction*
37. You should be confident that whatever   *The Customer*
    could have been done has been done to
    assure a maximum gratuity
38. It costs the Server no extra money and   *Introduction*
    only a very little extra time to change
    bad service to good service to
    superlative service
39. Insanity is not trying to increase   *Conclusion*
    your income
40. I have not come across one study yet   *Conclusion*
    that concludes that significant increases
    in tips cannot be achieved
41. The way I see it, our Server failed   *Introduction*
    to create a comfortable, friendly and
    relaxing experience
42. The diner has a basic expectation of   *Conclusion*
    good food and good service
43. What does the customer *really* want?   *Introduction*
44. I cannot argue with my own life's   *The Customer*
    experiences

45. ...each have their separate needs   *The Customer*

46. This book is unashamedly about you,   *Introduction*
the Server and how to make more
money for yourself – pure and simple

47. No matter what I do, the result will   *Conclusion*
always be the same. They won't tip

48. Remember, you cannot demand a tip.   *Conclusion*
You have to earn a tip

49. I guarantee   *Conclusion*

50. It is the perception of the customer   *The Server*
that counts. The customer is the one
who pays the bill, decides on and pays
the tip!

HERMAN®

by Jim Unger

9-25 © LaughingStock International Inc./dist. by United Media, 2003

"D'you mind if I take a photo? It's not often we get a 15-cent tip."

106

Reader Input

YOUR STORIES AND THOUGHTS ARE NEEDED

Well, enough about me – and my suggestions. I'd like to know how you are doing. There are numerous blogs for the vitriolic venting of all Server problems and, whilst these have their uses in airing common problems and generally 'letting off steam', I'm more interested in the 'good news' side of the profession.

What techniques have you found to be successful in increasing your tips?

What do you do to make your work more enjoyable?

Have you any funny, work-related stories that brightened your day and, maybe, increased your tips as well?

If you have any stories, anecdotes, tips, examples or nightmares that you'd like to share then please e-mail them to me through my web site at **www.howseverything.com.**

For those published, I will, of course, credit you with as much information as you can give me. I'd like to include some added character to your stories by personalizing them with as much information as you feel you'd like to give me. If, for any reason, you wish to remain anonymous then, of course, I'd be pleased to honour your request.

Selected References

Fast, Julius, *Body Language*, MJF Books, New York. 1970

Nierenberg, G.I., & Calero, H.H., *How to read a Person Like a Book*, Metro Books, New York. 1993

Morris, Desmond, *The Naked Ape*, Random House, New York. 1967

Morris Desmond, *The Human Zoo*, Kodansha America, New York. 1996

Van Baaren, R.B., Holland, RW Steenaert, B & van Knippenberg, A.

Mimicry for money: behavioural consequences of imitation. Journal of Experimental Social Psychology, 39, 393-398, (2003)

Nature News Service/Macmillan Magazine Ltd., 2003

William Shakespeare. *As You Like It*, Act 2 scene 7. 1479

How's Everything?

BY PETER STOKES

Trafford 2005, ISBN 1-4120-6012-5
Pricing* information in US and Canadian dollars

❏ Yes! I would like to order _____ copies of "How's Everything?" by Peter Stokes.

❏ Yes! I would like to speak with Peter about how his program can help our staff and company!

❏ Yes! I would like to interview Peter for an upcoming story we're working on!

❏ No. I would just like an autographed copy of the book for myself so I can learn how to make more money!

Shipping and payment information:

Name:_____

Address: _____

City: _____ Prov/State _____ Postal/ZIP _____

Telephone: _____ Fax:_____

E-mail: _____

Payment enclosed: ❏ Check   Credit Card   ❏ Visa ❏ MasterCard

Credit Card #:_____ Exp.Date:_____

Bank or Company Issuing Card:_____

Name on Card: _____

Cardholder's Address _____

City, Province/State,
Postal/Zip Associated w/Card: _____

*Bulk Purchase Discounts available.

Either e-mail order details to:
Peter@howseverything.com
mail to:
1680 Timberlands Road, Ladysmith, BC. Canada V9G 1K3
or fax to:
250-245-0801

About the Author

Peter Stokes was born in London, England and spent many years travelling the Globe while working within the Cabin Services Division of British Airways. This proved to be a wonderful opportunity for Peter to follow his passion for food, people and travel. He was continually fascinated by the many different countries and cultures visited and he vowed always to eat the food of the country he was in. That meant no hamburgers in Tokyo and no sushi in Nairobi – a rule he keeps to this day!

It was during these travels and dining in so many different restaurants, cafes, even shacks on the beach that the 'How's Everything?' bug was born and gradually evolved to the creation of this book.

On leaving the airline, Peter immigrated to Canada and settled in Vancouver, BC on the Pacific West coast. There followed many years of work, spent mainly in retail and other service industries, where Peter focused on the varied aspects of customer service, within management, as an independent consultant and a frequent lecturer. This work allowed him to continue his travels and people-meeting passion throughout Canada, the United States and Europe.

Peter now lives in Ladysmith on Vancouver Island where, with his wife, Lynnette, they own and manage the Timberland Pub and Restaurant. (www.timberlandpub.com)

ISBN 141206012-5

9 781412 060127